GOD'S MEDICINE

HOW TO RECEIVE DIVINE HEALING & KEEP IT

UEBERT ANGEL

LEVI HOUSE

ISBN 978-0-9558116-3-0

ONE
GOD AS YOUR DOCTOR

Proverbs 4:20-22 says, My son, attend to my words; incline thine ear unto my sayings. Let them not depart from thine eyes; keep them in the midst of thine heart. For they are life to those that find them, and HEALTH to all their flesh. (KJV)

The Hebrew word for "health" in verse 22 is 'Marpe' which means "literally a medicine or a cure." God's Word is actually a medicinal agent to all your flesh. It is the best medicine for you. It will cure any disease. It will heal you!

In fact the Lord adds to it by saying something very exciting, in the original Hebrew rendering of the bible, that he is a Medical Doctor. He says he is a Medical Practitioner.

This is proven in Exodus 15:26 when God says:

"...I am the Lord that HEALETH THEE..."

Isaac Leeser's translation of the same scripture, Exodus 15:26, reads:

"...I the Lord am thy PHYSICIAN..."

Did you see that? The word 'healeth" in Exodus 15:26 there is 'Rapha' which means 'Medical Doctor' or 'Medical Practitioner'. That scripture is calling God a Medical Doctor. It is taking God as your Medical Practitioner. It is not saying he will heal you only. It is claiming God is your GP.

The Lord says here, he is a Doctor and the medicine He prescribes is His Word. This Doctor who created you and the whole universe including all that is in it is saying He has His word as His medicine to cure and heal all your diseases.

Did you know that when an Israelite today is going to a Doctor he says I am going to the 'ro-FEH' which is exactly 'Rapha', the name God calls Himself by.

You see that God is not saying he is the Lord that 'healeth thee'. No not at all. He is making a bold statement that He is the Lord your GP. He is claiming to be your Doctor and nothing less. This is what they call the Doctor in Israel. God was using their day to day language and the translators of the bible went off the rails by that claim. To them it was too practical so the just put:

"I am the Lord that HEALETH THEE..."

Instead of saying it like God said it:

"I am the Lord your MEDICAL DOCTOR..."

Do you see that? Now you see that God is your GP. He is your Medical Practitioner. He is your Doctor. He can heal you if you take and follow his prescription!

Take God's Medicine Today

You can be healed today if you dare take this Doctor's medicine.

Many folks make the mistake of thinking its only believing that will bring healing. No, it's not only believing. Believing alone will give you a big smile whilst the Titanic is sinking. Expecting to be healed by saying 'I believe, I believe' will make you die with a good attitude.

Its just the same as singing 'twinkle, twinkle little star' and expect healing to come into your body. Some say its only confessing the word and they would still be dead wrong.

You hear them confess and say, "I believe in healing" without actually taking the medicine into your diseased body. It is all useless to just shout, "I believe in healing. I believe in healing" without taking in the medicine.

What benefit will it be for you to chew without swallowing? You would only stay hungry. What good is it to just see water without bathing? You will only be a dirty person. What good would it do for you to believe in food if you didn't eat it? You would starve. What good would it do for you to believe in water if you didn't actually drink any? You would remain thirsty.

Why would a patient go to the Doctor to hear the diagnosis and then take medicine home and sleep without swallowing or applying the medicine to their sick body?

You see you need to take the medicine of God for it to start working. God's Word is His medicine. It needs to be seen as medicine and be treated like you would pills BUT you need to start by trusting that God wants to heal everyone including you. That's where many people get stuck. They think **"maybe he wants to heal others but not me"** and that keeps them in sickness and chained in pain. They are just not sure if God wants to heal them.

Faith in the Medicine

Faith in this medicine is simple but key. Stay with me here.

Faith begins where the will of God is known. No matter how you take this medicine, if you don't understand that the Doctor is working with you and expecting you to live and knowing you will be helped, it would be difficult for you to be cured.

God Wants You Healed

As a believer you ought not to be sick. It is spiritually, morally, physically wrong for you to get sick. That is not your portion. Healing is your portion. It is the children's bread according to the Lord Jesus. He said to one woman:

Mark 7:27

How can I give THE CHILDREN'S BREAD (Healing) to dogs...

Jesus called 'Healing' the children's bread. In the time of Jesus and even today in Israel, BREAD is still the staple food so the Lord Jesus says HEALING IS AS COMMON AS STAPLE FOOD.

He declared that healing to him was as common as food. He took healing as something that even your own children have on a daily basis, FOOD. It is then easy and straightforward to assume that Jesus being good would be willing to give food to his children more than you are willing.

Only a bad father does not provide for his own family. Look at what the scripture says:

Luke 11:13

If you then being carnal know how to give good gifts to your children, how much more your father in heaven...

Watch this. You are also Abraham's seed and heirs according to the promise and you ought to be well. YOU ARE THE CHILD of the Lord and healing is your FOOD. It is your BREAD as the Lord Jesus said it.

Just take a look at what the Lord Jesus said when He was opposed for healing someone: Luke 13:16 records the response the Lord gave:

"And ought not this woman, being a daughter of Abraham, whom Satan hath bound, lo, these eighteen years, be loosed from this bond...?"

This is a divine FACT. It is not wishful thinking. It is beyond debate for the Lord says in effect:

"if you are ABRAHAM'S SEED (and you are) you have a birth right to get your healing"

See! If you are Abraham's seed, of which you are 100% according to Galatians 3:29, you do not have an option - you ought to be healed. You ought to be well. You can be healed. The Medicine will work for you. In fact it is designed to work for you.

If no person has told you yet that you are Abraham's seed then see what The Lord Jesus Himself through the Apostle Paul says in Galatians 3:29:

"If ye are Christ's then are ye Abraham's seed and heirs to the promise"

What promise? The promise that includes physical healing, but not limited to it, as is written in Luke 13:16 above.

As if that was not enough, we find the Apostle Peter saying you are not just going to be cured by this medicine only for the aforementioned reasons but among many reasons Peter says:

1 Peter 2:24

By his stripes ye were healed.

When people see this scripture they will say, 'no this is talking about spiritual healing' but they would be dead wrong. The scripture makes it clear. It leaves no doubt that God has done everything to heal all. He is not selecting a few people to get this healing. No, Healing is for all including you and when the bible says **"by his stripes ye were healed"** this is a physical healing it's talking about.

This is easy to see. Look at this:

> **Isaiah 53:4**
>
> **Surely he has borne our grief's and carried our sorrows; yet we esteemed Him stricken, smitten by God, and afflicted.**

In Matthew 8 Verses 16-17 says:

> **"When evening had come, they brought to Him many who were demon-possessed. And He cast out the spirits with a word, and HEALED ALL who were sick, that it might be FULFILLED which was spoken by Isaiah the prophet, saying: "He Himself took our infirmities and bore our sicknesses."**

Isaiah was dealing with the truth that since Jesus died for you, you are receiving your healing. Do you see that this healing is real. Do you see that the Lord is the word of God and healing is with his word. His word is Medicine. Have faith and know God wants to heal everyone, INCLUDING YOU!

He is going to do this through his healing agent, His Word.

Healing Agent

God's Word is a healing agent, just as natural medicine is a healing agent. In other words, the medicine itself contains the capacity to produce healing. It has the power to cure any disease. God's word has power to destroy sickness if you dare take it as a medicinal agent.

You know if a medicine like 'quinine' gets into your body you don't have to help it or speak to it to work or shout for it to work. No you don't. It won't even hear you because inherent within God's Word is the capacity, the energy, the ability, and the nature to effect healing in your body. It will not need your help. What is required of you is to take the prescription and take the medicine well.

The other nice thing about this healing agent or medicine that ought to be mentioned is, it is free and it has already been sent to you free of charge from God.

Psalm 107:20 concurs:

He sent his word, and healed them, and delivered them from their destructions.

This is exactly what the main text, Proverbs 4:22 says:

For they (God's Medicine, His Words) are life unto those that find them, and health to all their flesh.

Isaiah 55:11 also agrees:

"The Word of God will accomplish what it was sent out to do."

And what was it send to do? The answer is very simple. It was sent to be

"...HEALTH to ALL YOUR FLESH..."

Not 'some' of your flesh but

"...ALL YOUR FLESH..."

The Word itself contains the power to produce what it says. Just as medicine has power to do what it says on the tin. Remember when God said, "Let there be light" and there was light. When he said 'let there be trees" there were trees and until this day, trees are there and the light is still shining. Healing Scriptures in God's word contain within them the capacity to produce healing and if you stick to the word you will definitely come back with a testimony.

Psalm 138:2 says of the word of God:

"...for he has magnified HIS WORD above His name..."

This tells you how powerful the word of God, which is God's medicine, is to you. It is bigger than the name of God which is above all names. It is big. It will do what it says it will do. Believe it and drink it. Believe it and swallow it. Make it the standard for your life and it will heal you. You don't need to help it when it gets into you, it will work inside you on its own and healing will be yours!

Hebrews 4:12

For the word of God is quick and powerful, and sharper than any two-edged sword, piercing even to the dividing asunder of soul and spirit ... (KJV)

God's Message is full of life and power. (Weymouth)

God's Word is alive with energy. (Jordan)

God's word to us is something alive, full of energy. (Knox)

The key to partaking of the life and healing energy in the Word is feeding on it until it penetrates your spirit where it deposits that life and energy.

We might say that medicine is no respecter of persons. It will work for anyone who takes it. It is not a matter of 'if' God is willing or not willing to heal any individual, but whether or not the individual will receive healing by taking the medicine that produces it.

God Has to Be Believed Just as You Would a Doctor

Many believers would believe a Doctor more than God. They would go under the knife on an operating table with a Doctor in a mask and holding knives and are never afraid. The Doctor they have never met. They will not have seen the results of his work but they will give him the right to cut their body and try to fix things without any reservations from them.

Now watch this:

2 Chronicles 16:12

And Asa in the thirty and ninth year of his reign was diseased in his feet, until his disease was exceeding great; yet in his disease he sought not to the LORD, but to the physicians...AND HE DIED.

Asa trusted in Doctors more than God and it killed him. Let it be noted that I am not saying a Doctor should not be believed. Luke in the Bible was a Doctor but believed in God's healing power so much that he followed and became a disciple of Apostle Paul, a healing minister.

You see God will meet you at the level of your faith. If your faith in God is too low with regards to a specific ailment then a Doctor will have to suffice. All I am saying is there is something better than the Doctor's medicine and it is God's word, which is His medicine.

You see this is dangerous for you to trust a doctor and not trust the God who created this vast universe and all that is in them. The same God says he has his medicine that can heal you and he is the logical healer because he is the one who made you so he knows when something is wrong with you.

Take In God's Medicine Now!

Now do you see that the best way to get God's word to work in your life is to take it like medicine?

If the DOCTOR tells you to take your medicine THREE TIMES a day then you need to read these verses at least three times a day and if you agree then try this same word of God which is His medicine at least three times a day or more and see what God's medicine will do for you.

TWO
SWALLOW GOD'S MEDICINE

The main thing with God's medicine is it works well when it is taken internally. Just like pills are swallowed in order to work so does the word of God. It must be taken internally.

You see, medicine must be taken according to directions that the doctor gives you for it to be effective. You can't just say,

" I know I should take medicine two times per day according to the doctor but who cares he said twice I will do only one per week".

That will not be wise. You can't say,

"The doctor is crazy to tell me to rub this medicine on my skin I would rather drink it"

You can die of that disease if you think that way. You see follow what is on the tin or what the doctor says. Follow the doctor's prescription. It is what will work.

Follow the Doctor's Prescription

Sometimes you go to see the Doctor or visit the pharmacist and you are given medicine labeled, "Take externally" or simply "Take internally." When it says 'internally' it would be down right madness to rub it on your body externally when the directions explicitly say to take it internally, it will not work. To take it after meals when the directions say take it before meals will reduce its effectiveness. To take it once in a while when the directions say three times a day will mean limited results, if any.

No matter how good the medicine is, it must be taken according to the directions or it won't work. So it is with God's medicine. It must be taken according to directions for it to work.

God's Prescription for Healing You

There are directions for taking God's medicine. God is the Physician and Doctor and has given specifications with regards to how to take His medicine. God's medicine itself will work if you will get it inside of you.

This is why the bible in Proverbs 4:20-22 says,

> **"My son, attend to my words; incline thine ear unto my sayings. Let them not depart from thine eyes; keep them in the midst of thine heart. For they are life to those that find them, and health to all their flesh."(KJV)**

The words **"…Attend to my words…"** mean 'attend to my prescription' or 'follow my prescription'. The Doctor is here telling you to listen to the prescription.

The word here says:

"…Let them (God's Medicine) not depart from thine eyes; keep them in the midst of thine heart…"

You see here that the word of God, which is God's Medicine, has to be kept in the heart. Not just in the heart but in the…

"…midst of your heart…"

To enter the midst of your heart requires your constant meditation on the medicine. You have to have a mind that agrees that the medicine works. To do that your eyes have to be fixed on the inerrant and sufficient word of God.

"…Let them not depart from thine eyes; keep them in the midst of thine heart…"

Keeping this medicine of God before your eyes causes the Word to get into the midst of your heart. It is only when God's Words get in through your eyes and through your mouth that it enters the midst of your heart and stay there that's when they produce healing in your body.

God's medicine has to penetrate your spirit through meditation – attending, hearing, looking, muttering, musing, and pondering – to produce healing in your body. But once they do penetrate, they will surely bring health to ALL YOUR FLESH. Let them penetrate deep within your heart and you will receive a testimony.

No Overdose With God's Medicine

The good thing about this medicine is there is nothing called an overdose. In fact if satisfactory results are not obtained right away or symptoms do not leave, you can double the dosage, treble or even quadruple the dosage without the fear of over dosing yourself to death. Do you see that you can take God's Word as a medicine with no danger of overdosing yourself?

The other thing is you do not have to buy it. It is free!

Whatever sickness or disease you are suffering from, God's Word can cure it. It is effective for any condition. There is no disease God's medicine cannot heal. No sickness it cannot destroy and no pain it cannot stop.

However for this medicine to work for you, remember the most important thing we have said in Chapter one: like any medicine, God's Word has to be taken to be effective. It will not work sitting on the shelf. And it has to be taken according to the directions. If you will follow God's directions as faithfully as you would follow the directions of a human doctor, you will see wonderful results.

Here Are the Directions & Prescription

PROVERBS 4:20-23 NKJ takes us right into the heart of the directions.

Proverbs 4:20-23

20 My son, give attention to my words; incline your ear to my sayings.

21 Do not let them depart from your eyes; keep them in the midst of your heart;

22 For they are life to those who find them, and health to all their flesh.

23 Keep your heart with all diligence, for out of it spring the issues of life.

As you have already seen in verse 22 the Hebrew word translated *health* is translated as *medicine* or cure. This is supported in scripture and here are just some of the scriptures that deal with the proof that the medicine exists.

PSALM 107:20 NKJV

He sent His word and healed them, and delivered them from their destructions.

Notice what it says right there. It says God's Word will heal. It is full of God's power and carries the authority of God who spoke it.

God's Word will not return to God void, but will produce what He sent it to do.

JOHN 8:31-32 NKJV

Then Jesus said to those Jews who believed Him, If you abide in My word, you are My

disciples indeed. And you shall know the truth, and the truth shall make you free.

You have the guarantee of Jesus. There is no better guarantee than the guarantee of Jesus. He is the GREAT Physician. His word is sure and his word is sufficient and inerrant in its nature. His Word will produce healing for you. That's a Jesus guarantee. But, you must continue in His Word, which is his medicine.

You must feed on it in until you know that you know, that you know, deep down in your knower that the truth has now reached your flesh. Then you will act on that Truth and it will make you free. Remember it is not the truth, that make you free. No, its not. It is the truth that you know!

God's medicine in verse 32 says:

John 8:32

...you shall KNOW the truth and the truth shall make you free...

The truth you know shall make you a magnet to healing and to know the truth like aforementioned you take it into your inner being. You do that by listening to the Word, reading the Word, and speaking the Word on a daily basis to yourself. Remember there is no overdose here. Filling your thoughts with the Word of God more than anything else is the key. The more of God's medicine you take, the better off you will be!

Many believers suffer from what they know which is contrary to the word of God so in this instance they need more portions of this medicine. They need to keep drinking or taking in this medicine and since there is no overdose, all is well. It is a risk free zone.

You just need to remove doubt and you will be on your way to health.

Doubt Is A Pathogenic Bacteria

Many ask me how do I remove doubt. It's easy. It is written for you in our main text:

PROVERBS 4:20-23 NKJ

20 My son, give attention to my words; incline your ear to my sayings.

21 Do not let them depart from your eyes; keep them in the midst of your heart;

22 For they are life to those who find them, and health to all their flesh.

23 Keep your heart with all diligence, for out of it spring the issues of life.

Verse 23 gives a way to remove doubt from the midst of your heart where the medicine will work from. You see the midst of your heart is like a laboratory with medicine and doctors working on your sickness and there they do not need their medicine to be mixed with any foreign thing like doubt.

In order to be able not to mess things up for yourself, get people who talk negatively out of your life. It is important not to be acquainted with negative reports whether from friends or from the doctor.

Have you seen that when many people hear that they have cancer, H.I.V or any other disease, they immediately resign from life and within weeks of being informed by the doctor their health deteriorates? It's mainly because, they know from reports that these diseases are killers. They heard from someone but they have not yet consulted the word of God, which says something completely different.

Medical reports on the type of disease they have tells them what to believe and if it says this is an incurable disease that's what they will have in the midst of their heart so it disturbs God's medicine from working effectively.

LOOK AT WHAT IT SAYS IN THE FOLLOWING VERSES. IT SAYS KEEP YOUR HEART WITH DILIGENCE... be wise who you listen to because what you hear may affect you or effect great change in your taking of God's medicine.

Here we are not saying we deny the fact that you are sick or your loved one is sick. No we are not denying the fact but WE HAVE THE TRUTH, and the TRUTH overrides the facts.

We have God's medicine which is free and which is true.

The Injection or Syringe for God's Medicine

Medicine is administered orally or through a syringe directly into your blood system. When administered orally the medicine has to go through your digestive system but ultimately will end up in your blood system.

Now **Homologia** is the injection for God's medicine, straight into your spirit. Homologia is a Greek compound word made up of two words, Homo, which means same and Logia, which is from logos which means Gods written word. It goes beyond acknowledging the word, it means to internalize the same word which God has spoken to you. It means to say the same thing as another, by way of agreement. You agree by professing, which means to declare openly, speak out freely the same word which God has spoken concerning your life.

This profession should be maintained irrespective of the situation on the ground. Just like a doctor who prescribes medicine three times a day, the medicine is taken even if symptoms persist. The problem with most folks is that when they see the symptoms, they stop the confessions yet with the medicine they take up until the tin of pills is empty. Watch this:

Hebrews 10:23

"Let us hold fast the profession of our faith without wavering; (for he is FAITHFUL that promised)."

The word **'fast'** there means, firmly fixed as in roots fast in the ground, it means to adhere firmly, not easily freed, unmovable and unshakable. Do sick people stop taking medicine when they see the symptoms not going away? No, they are a stickler to the prescription until the tin is thrown away. This is the level of trust you must develop in Gods word, hold fast despite what the devil throws at you.

You need to hold fast the profession of your faith, the word 'profession' is the word **'homologia'**, as we dealt with earlier, it means saying the same word which God is talking about your situation. What God says are his promises and he is faithful to deliver what he has promised because he has placed his word above himself. God is faithful, which means he sticks to the prescription of his word, but the question now is, are you also a stickler to the prescription? Are you unwavering in the face of symptoms, Doctors reports and when you feel pain in your flesh? These are facts but is the truth which you confess going to be unwavering in the face of adversity?

One Woman's Testimony from the Bible

The bible talks about an unwavering woman who stood firm upon Gods word, defying tradition, culture and custom. Instead she held fast onto the profession of her unconscious faith and kept saying what God had promised.

My bible puts it this way:

Malachi 4:2

...But unto you that fear my name shall the Sun of righteousness arise with healing in his wings...

This verse is like finding yourself inside a pharmaceutical dispensary, where you are swamped with diverse prescriptions for the same ailment, to the extent that you don't know which one to choose. You see, Malachi the Prophet was prophesying about the long awaited Messiah who was to illuminate and impute righteousness on each and every believer, but that was not all he was to bring. His wings, which refers to the hem of the garment of Jesus Christ was to be endowed with healing medicine. Not so much the garment but Jesus Christ would be so endowed with healing anointing to the extent that even his garments will be so saturated that healing, **marpe**, which we defined earlier as medicine' will naturally be there.

The woman with the issue of blood had so much against her, bleeding profusely and continuously for 12 years is no small thing. Not only was her blood hemorrhaging, but even her money was being drained by doctors as she sought help. In the Jewish culture this was considered as uncleanliness and such people were supposed to be quarantined until their problem was rectified.

Leviticus 15:19

And if a woman have an issue, and her issue in her flesh be blood, she shall be put apart seven days: and whosoever toucheth her shall be unclean until the even.

So not only was she unclean but whosoever touches her would also be deemed unclean. Do you see what she was up against, the Law required her to be set apart, not to mix with people for 7 days, yet she had been bleeding for 12 years. The bible shows us how unwavering she was, AGAINST ALL ODDS:

Matthew 9:20-21

And behold, a woman, which was diseased with an issue of blood twelve years, came behind him, and touched the hem of his garment.

For she said within herself, if I may but touch his garment, I shall be whole.

She bulldozed her way through and sneaked from behind to touch the hem of the garment of Jesus. But you may ask, why the hem, why not anywhere else. This is because of the scripture we read earlier on, where Malachi prophesied that marpe, medicine will be on the wings of the Sun of Righteousness, so there was medicine on Jesus, boy I love Jesus. She was just following the prescription given by the Doctor from heaven in Malachi.

However she did something before she touched the hem of the garment, **"...she said to herself**..." which means, she kept on professing, saying the same thing which had been prophesied by Malachi, she was in agreement with that promise so she was in **'homologia'** with the word and kept on saying it, even though tradition and the Mosaic Law said she shouldn't be near men, she held on **'fast'** to her medicine, the word and kept agreeing. More importantly she acted upon what she believed, that's 'unconscious faith', she ignored or became unconscious of the laws in Leviticus and sneaked through until she grabbed the hem of the garment where her promise was.

At that moment of contact, Jesus turned and asked 'who touched me', the disciples went into defensive mode and retorted that many have been touching you for a multitude not only thronged him but also pressed against him. So many made contact, but were not able to draw out virtue, healing power from his wings.

It takes meditation of the word, sticking to the prescription even in the face of adversity for you to receive the promise. She kept on saying to herself, if only I could touch his garment, she kept on taking in her medicine even though she saw a multitude of men who she was not supposed to intermingle with.

You see she was able to stick to the word, which is God's medicine against all odds. She kept the **'homologia'**. She did not stop talking about her healing. She continued taking her medicine until her healing.

Don't stop taking your prescription, the healing word, because of a Doctors report or because of pain for:

2 Corinthians 5:7

...We do not walk by sight or sensory perception but we walk by faith.

Jesus then said, **'your faith has made you whole'** and she was immediately healed.

Now, before we talk more about faith, I want to walk with you through the war chest of medicine in the dispensary of the Sun of Righteousness, whose wings are endowed with marpe, medicine. Just stay with me here and you will see how your healing is guaranteed!

THREE
GOD'S MEDICINE CABINET

Have you noticed how some folks have all sorts of medicines in their Cabinet's, with an assortment of drugs for headaches, from experience they now even know which one dissolves pain faster and which ones have side effects.

God also has a cabinet, with a war chest of capsules, which contain marpe, it also has prescriptions on how often the capsules should be taken. If circumstances grow worse, all you need to do is double the dosage.

Here is the prescription:

> **This book of the law shall not depart out of thy mouth; but thou shalt meditate therein day and night, that thou mayest observe to do according to all that is written therein: for then thou shalt make thy way prosperous, and then thou shalt have good success.**
>
> **Joshua 1:8**

The medicine is to be taken twice per day, day and night by way of meditation and the word is to be spoken three times a day until faith comes, then once a day to maintain faith. If symptoms grow worse, double, treble, quadruple the dosage and guaranteed, there are no side effects. The results are guaranteed, you will prosper and have good success in your health, but only if you observe to do according to the prescription.

I have handpicked scriptures from the word for your medication and need to be swallowed up by you by means of '**homologia**'. You have to say these scriptures and confessions to yourself. Meditate on them. Ponder them in your heart. Speak them out loud over yourself in the first person, laying claim to them by faith, with the understanding that as a born-again child of God, *the Word of God is your inheritance*. Use them in praise to your Heavenly Father! His Word is medicine to all your flesh!

Doctors may have told you there is no more hope for you medically, but you can always find Supernatural Hope – a goal setter and Supernatural Faith – a goal getter, from God's word, his medicine for you.

In his cabinet there is a war chest of medicine, from pain killers, immune system boosters, so that no sickness can come near you and even specific medicine for specific diseases.

Here Is How You Do It

Here is where you need to listen very intently. You do not get medicine from a Doctor so that you take it back to him. That would be silly. Medicine, is given by a Doctor so that you the patient can apply it to the diseased body. That is what makes sense. You see, you cannot take God's word and beg God to heal you with it. No, you don't. A good patient applies medicine to the diseased body. You take the medicine of God's word to your sickness and apply God's medicine to your DISEASED BODY.

The medicine you see below should be taken or rather confessed three times a day. If symptoms do not leave at the desired time, increase the dosage. Always remember the more the dosage, the better the results.

The great minister of the Gospel, Marylyn Hickey, did it twenty four times a day and her cancerous growth fell off. I have used it often and my wife has used it often and we have not been disappointed. I have taught these principles and too many people have been enjoying their results and still are. The medicine from God works. It is guaranteed!

You need to speak this word loudly and believe in your heart that this medicine of God works. Speak it to yourself. Don't stop talking about it. Confess it until symptoms leave and when you are healed it means you will have received divine healing yet there is another level you attain called divine health which can prevent you from ever being afflicted by a disease. That level is obtained by continually speaking this word over your body so as to block any disease from coming in.

This medicine as you see will also act as a preventative measure for viruses, bacteria and an foreign body if repeated daily even after you receive your healing.

I have put for you areas of confession so that they can help you in your taking of your medicine, which is God's Word.

Speak them to yourself and do not just select your disease only and say this is my category so all others do not matter. That will be a mistake. Speak and confess all this to your body for better results.

Remember you are only using three times a day as minimum dosage. To get maximum results from this medicine requires double dosage or more. Remember there are no side effects and the more the dosage, the better the results. NOW take your medicine as has been prescribed!

Growth, Lumps, Tumors and Arthritis

For verily I say unto you, That whosoever shall say unto this mountain, Be thou removed, and be thou cast into the sea; and shall not doubt in his heart, but shall believe that those things which he saith shall come to pass; he shall have whatsoever he saith.

Mark 11:23

Confession

Jesus bore the curse for me: therefore I forbid growths and tumors to inhabit my body. The life of God in me dissolves Growths, Tumors and Arthritis, they are uprooted and removed without trace. My strength is renewed and my health is restored in the name of Jesus.

Hebrews 4:12

For the word of God is quick, and powerful, and sharper than any two edged sword,

piercing even to the dividing asunder of soul and spirit, and of the joints and marrow, and is a discerner of the thoughts and intents of the heart.

Confession

The word of God is sharper than any two edged sword, therefore it is sharper than any surgical knife, if it can separate the soul and spirit, joints and marrow, today it cuts away any Growth, lump, tumor and arthritis without trace. I am made whole in the name of Jesus.

Heart, Arteries and Blood

Proverbs 14:30

A sound heart is the life of the flesh: but envy the rottenness of the bones.

Thanks Giving Declaration

Father I thank you, that I have a strong and sound heart, it beats with the rhythm of your spirit. My blood flows to every cell at the right pressure my body is vitalized I have the God kind of life in me.

Psalm 4:7-8

Thou hast put gladness in my heart, more than in the time that their corn and their wine increased. I will both lay me down in peace, and sleep: for thou, LORD, only makest me dwell in safety.

Prophetic Declaration

My heart is flooded with love, I have gladness in my heart, I have no heart aches or stress, my blood pressure is 120/80, my blood sugar and iron level are normal for the life of God flows in my body and cleanses my arteries of any excess fat or corruption in my blood. I am at peace, I am at ease awake or in sleep, Thank God I have been made safe. In the Name of Jesus Christ.

Body Tissue and Cells

Romans 8:11

But if the Spirit of him that raised up Jesus from the dead dwell in you, he that raised up Christ from the dead shall also quicken your mortal bodies by his Spirit that dwelleth in you.

Confession

The Spirit of God dwells inside me, I am the embassy of the Holy Spirit, any dead, frail and weak body tissue and cells are being quickened. They are made alive, I am invigorated and am springing up with the God kind of life. In the name of Jesus.

Matthew 12:25

And Jesus knew their thoughts, and said unto them, Every kingdom divided against itself is brought to desolation; and every city or house divided against itself shall not stand:

Prophetic Declaration

I place an embargo upon any foreign tissue or cells in my body, I remove any foreign elements in my tissue and cells. Any virus, bacteria or infirmity, your lease is over. My body is whole, no sickness can divide it. My body is sound, life and health is mine today, in the name of Jesus Christ.

Healthy Bones and Marrow

Proverbs 16:24

Pleasant words are as an honeycomb, sweet to the soul, and health to the bones.

Confession

I speak life to my bones and joints of my body. I declare and decree I am sound and strong. Word of God, you are my pleasant medicine to my bones and marrow, in the name of Jesus.

Proverbs 17:22

A merry heart doeth good like a medicine: but a broken spirit drieth the bones.

Confession

My heart is full of the word, I have received love shed into my heart. My heart is merry, it is like medicine, I have joy for my spirit is strengthened. My bones and marrow are made whole. In the name of Jesus.

Ulcers, Depression and Stress

Philippians 4:6

Be careful for nothing; but in everything by prayer and supplication with thanksgiving let your request be made known unto God.

Confession

I am careful for nothing, anxiety is not my portion, I have a father who knows my prayers and supplication before I say them. I give my thanksgiving today for my requests have been heard and he always answers with a YES. In the name of Jesus.

Matthew 6:25

Take no thought for your life, what ye shall eat, or what ye shall drink; nor yet for your body, what ye shall put on. Is not the life more than meat, and the body than raiment.

I take no thought about tomorrow because my God is my provider, He is my more than enough and He orders my steps. I have no stress about provision and clothing for I am made whole by the blood of Jesus.

Paralysis

Acts 9:34

And Peter said unto him, Aeneas, Jesus Christ maketh thee whole: arise, and make thy bed. And he arose immediately.

And

Mark 2:11

I say unto thee, Arise, and take up thy bed, and go thy way into thine house.

Confession

I receive strength in my bones and muscles. My ligaments and sinews receive strength from on High. I am vitalized, I am strengthened for I have the power and energy of God inside me. I can do all things by Christ who strengthens me. In the name of Jesus Christ.

Cancer, STD, HIV and AIDS

Psalm 38:7

For my loins are filled with a loathsome disease: and there is no soundness in my flesh.

Confession

By the stripes of Jesus I am healed, I have soundness in my flesh. I am made whole in the name of Jesus.

Deuteronomy 28:27,35

The Lord will smite thee with the botch of Egypt, and with the emerods, and with the scab, and with the itch, whereof thou canst not be healed.

The Lord shall smite thee in the knees, and in the legs, with a sore botch that cannot be healed, from the sole of thy foot unto the top of thy head.

And

Galatians 3:13

Christ hath redeemed us from the curse of the law, being made a curse for us: for it is written, Cursed is every one that hangeth on a tree.

Confession

I am bought at a price, I am redeemed from the curse of the law, all sickness and disease including which Doctors say cannot be cured were nailed on the cross. Cancer, HIV, STD and AIDS was nailed on the cross, I receive my healing in the name of Jesus Christ.

Immune System

Job 1:10

Hast not thou made an hedge about him, and about his house, and about all that he hath on every side? thou hast blessed the work of his hands, and his substance is increased in the land.

Prophetic Declaration

I have a supernatural hedge around me, my immune system is quickened and strengthened, no virus or bacteria can enter, I am a Jesus Zone no sickness can enter. I speak life to my immune system, in the name of Jesus Christ.

Isaiah 59:19

So shall they fear the name of the LORD from the west, and his glory from the rising of the sun. When the enemy shall come in like a flood, the Spirit of the LORD shall lift up a standard against him.

Prophetic Declaration

My Immune System is lifted up, my white blood cells are multiplied, my lymphatic system is lifted up no pathogen, bug, plague or epidemic can enter for God has raised my blood count. My immune system is intact, no sickness can enter. I am Heavily defended and Heavily guarded in the name of Jesus Christ.

Further Scriptures and Notes for Meditation, Confessions and Declarations

Exodus 15:26

And said, If thou wilt diligently hearken to the voice of the LORD thy God, and wilt do that which is right in his sight, and wilt give ear to his commandments, and keep all his statutes, I will put none of these diseases upon thee, which I have brought upon the Egyptians: for I am the LORD that healeth thee.

Confession

God is speaking to me now, saying, "I am the LORD that healeth thee." He is watching over His Word to perform it. He is the LORD that healeth me. He is healing me now. This Word contains the ability to produce what it says. His Word is full of healing power. I receive this Word now. Healing is God's nature. God is in me. My body is the temple of the LORD that healeth me. God is bigger than sickness and Satan. God is dwelling inside of me, healing me now.

Exodus 23:25

And ye shall serve the LORD your God, and he shall bless thy bread, and thy water; and I will take sickness away from the midst of thee.

Note

True worship from the heart is a key to walking in divine health. Close every door you can to the devil.

Deuteronomy 7:15

And the LORD will take away from thee all sickness, and will put none of the evil diseases of Egypt, which thou knowest, upon thee; but will lay them upon all them that hate thee.

Note

The scripture says, ALL not some, there is no sickness which Dr Jesus, can't remove. Science tells us that some viruses can't be cured, some can only be managed but this is not what the prescription is saying. All sickness, that includes cancer, HIV, paralysis or any terminal disease you can think of.

Deuteronomy 28:1-14

1 And it shall come to pass, if thou shalt hearken diligently unto the voice of the LORD thy God, to observe and to do all his commandments which I command thee this day, that the LORD thy God will set thee on high above all nations of the earth: 2 And all these blessings shall come on thee, and overtake thee, if thou shalt hearken unto the voice of the LORD thy God. 3 Blessed shalt thou be in the city, and blessed shalt thou be

in the field. 4 Blessed shall be the fruit of thy body, and the fruit of thy ground, and the fruit of thy cattle, the increase of thy kine, and the flocks of thy sheep. 5 Blessed shall be thy basket and thy store. 6 Blessed shalt thou be when thou comest in, and blessed shalt thou be when thou goest out. 7 The LORD shall cause thine enemies that rise up against thee to be smitten before thy face: they shall come out against thee one way, and flee before thee seven ways. 8 The LORD shall command the blessing upon thee in thy storehouses, and in all that thou settest thine hand unto; and he shall bless thee in the land which the LORD thy God giveth thee. 9 The LORD shall establish thee an holy people unto himself, as he hath sworn unto thee, if thou shalt keep the commandments of the LORD thy God, and walk in his ways. 10 And all people of the earth shall see that thou art called by the name of the LORD; and they shall be afraid of thee. 11 And the LORD shall make thee plenteous in goods, in the fruit of thy body, and in the fruit of thy cattle, and in the fruit of thy ground, in the land which the LORD sware unto thy fathers to give thee. 12 The LORD shall open unto thee his good treasure, the heaven to give the rain unto thy land in his season, and to bless all the work of thine hand: and thou shalt lend unto many nations, and thou shalt not borrow. 13 And the LORD shall make thee the

head, and not the tail; and thou shalt be above only, and thou shalt not be beneath; if that thou hearken unto the commandments of the LORD thy God, which I command thee this day, to observe and to do them: 14 And thou shalt not go aside from any of the words which I command thee this day, to the right hand, or to the left, to go after other gods to serve them.

Notice

The blessing of the Lord is your's, all you need to do is to 'hearken' to his voice. To hearken is to listen, not as a hearer but one who listens in order to do. Confess his word, and more importantly Act upon it. For confession without possession is faith at a junior level. It's only when you Act upon it, that when your confession becomes possession.

Deuteronomy 30:19-20

19 I call heaven and earth to record this day against you, that I have set before you life and death, blessing and cursing: therefore choose life, that both thou and thy seed may live: 20 That thou mayest love the LORD thy God, and that thou mayest obey his voice, and that thou mayest cleave unto him: for he is thy life, and the length of thy days: that thou mayest dwell in the land which the LORD sware unto thy fathers, to Abraham, to Isaac, and to Jacob, to give them.

Notice

The choice has been laid before you, there is no reason for you to suffer yet your healing is a done deal. Choose life, choose divine healing, choose to take your prescription today which will usher you into a life of no sickness.

Joshua 21:45

There failed not ought of any good thing which the LORD had spoken unto the house of Israel; all came to pass.

Note

How much more sure is this promise to us since our covenant with God is based upon the shed Blood of Jesus Christ! Healing is a good gift from God!

1 Kings 8:56

Blessed be the LORD, that hath given rest unto his people Israel, according to all that he promised: there hath not failed one word of all his good promise, which he promised by the hand of Moses his servant.

Note

Not even a single word failed, of the promises God made to the people of Israel, because God has placed his word above himself.

2 Chronicles 7:14

If my people, which are called by my name, shall humble themselves, and pray, and seek my face, and turn from their wicked ways; then will I hear from heaven, and will forgive their sin, and will heal their land.

Note

Prayer, 'prosuche' in the greek, is when you fill your spirit with God's word, your prescription and then send it back to him in prayer. Instead of repeating your complaints which have not yielded healing, repent from evil ways by confessing your sins, he is more than ready to forgive you, by the blood of Jesus they have been washed away hence healing is your portion.

Job 5:26

Thou shalt come to thy grave in a full age, like as a shock of corn cometh in his season.

And

Psalm 91:16

With long life will I satisfy him, and shew him my salvation.

Note

Refuse to die young and full of potential, full age is your portion, you shall not die young, death is swallowed by life, sickness is swallowed by health, this is your portion, make it your prescription for meditation, confess it by mouth and full age will become your portion. Declare it even for your children, born or still to be born. Long life is your portion, it doesn't matter even if in your generation or family people die young, the curse is broken by the word.

Psalm 30:2

O LORD my God, I cried unto thee, and thou hast healed me.

Notice

It is his will to heal you, there is no such thing as maybe he doesn't want to heal me or he is teaching me a lesson by sickness. Cry out to him in prayer and receive your promise of healing. His ears are open to hear you, pray, pray, pray, pray!!!

Psalms 34:7

The angel of the LORD encampeth round about them that fear him, and delivereth them.

Confession

I have angels of the Lord around me, no sickness can enter, I am a Jesus Zone, no demon or sickness can enter for I am God protected. In the name of Jesus Christ.

Psalm 34:19

Many are the afflictions of the righteous: but the LORD delivereth him out of them all.

Notice

Though the Doctor has said I have this ailement, I am not ignorant of the devil's devices for I know, I am aware that the Lord will deliver me from ALL not some but ALL of them. The root cause of sickness is uprooted, the symptoms are removed in the name of Jesus.

Psalm 41:3

The LORD will strengthen him upon the bed of languishing [sickness]: thou wilt make [restore] all his bed in his sickness.

Prophetic Declaration

This is not my death bed, I refuse to die on this bed before I complete my divine assignment, I receive power today from the Lord who heals me, I receive miracle working power and strength, I have strength in my bones and flesh from the sole of my feet to the crown of my head, in the name of Jesus Christ.

Psalm 42:11

Why art thou cast down, O my soul? and why art thou disquieted within me? hope thou in God: for I shall yet praise him, who is the health of my countenance, and my God.

Confession

I refuse to be cast down for there is a lifting up, my spirit is up and it lifts up my soul and body for I have the power and energy of God inside me. I choose today to praise Him, with thanks giving, for you are my Physician, my Healer and my God. In the name of Jesus Christ.

Psalms 91:1

He that dwelleth in the secret place of the most High shall abide under the shadow of the Almighty.

Note

The word shadow in the Hebrew is the word 'Tsel', which is the word 'Epikaizo' in the Greek, that is the highest dimension of power, his boiling point which defies natural laws. It's the same word used when Peters shadow would heal people in the street.

Confession

I dwell, under the shadow of the Almighty, natural laws of sickness, epidemics and viruses are defied because of the Shadow, the Epikaizo of God. The Doctors report is overshadowed, the pain is overshadowed, the symptoms are overshadowed and the root problem is overshadowed. I am healed, by the stripes of Jesus Christ, I am healed. In the name of Jesus.

Psalms 91:9-10

9 Because thou hast made the LORD, which is my refuge, even the most High, thy habitation; 10 There shall no evil befall thee, neither shall any plague come nigh thy dwelling.

Notice

A plague is an epidemic disease which causes a high rate of deaths. It used to be Influenza some ages ago, it was once small pox, then chicken pox, malaria causes havoc in some regions, these days it's things like Blood Pressure, Diabetes, Obesity, HIV, Aids and several cancers.

These are the facts, but not the truth. The truth is none of these plagues, epidemics will touch you, because you are protected. That should be your confession.

Psalms 103:2-3

2 Bless the LORD, O my soul, and forget not all his benefits: 3 Who forgiveth all thine iniquities; who healeth all thy diseases;

Note

Notice it doesn't say some, it says all! It also states that healing is one of the benefits that belongs to the believer along with the benefit of having our sin forgiven.

Psalm 105:37

He brought them forth also with silver and gold: and there was not one feeble person among their tribes.

Note

Bible scholars estimate that there were about 2.5 million Israelites who left Egypt healed, healthy, and whole. This is after captivity and enslavement for 400 years! This was and still is God's will for His people today? All healed, healthy, and whole, regardless of your current situation. This is His will!

Psalms 107:19-20

19 Then they cry unto the LORD in their trouble, and he saveth them out of their distresses. 20 He sent his word, and healed them, and delivered them from their destructions.

Notice

His word is all you need, for it is marpe, it is medicine, take the word to heart, seize it and act upon it.

Psalm 118:17

I shall not die, but live, and declare the works of the LORD.

Note: Agree with this right now! Declare it with your voice! God has a plan for your life here on the Earth. Don't let the enemy steal it away. You can do what God says you can do, you can be what God says you can be! Cast down those thoughts and imaginations that don't line up with the Word of God!

Psalm 119:50

This is my comfort in my affliction: for thy word hath quickened me.

Note

The word quickened means to keep alive, to nourish up, to restore, to revive to health or life, from faintness, sickness and even death. May these words comfort you and vitalize you to life today.

Proverbs 3:7-8

7 Be not wise in thine own eyes: fear the LORD, and depart from evil. 8 It shall be health to thy navel, and marrow to thy bones.

Note

The term "fear the LORD" means to reverence and worship the LORD in all things. Such worship and Holiness is medicine to your navel, which means your abdomen and to your bones. No bone cancer, arthritis, swollen ligaments, abdominal pains can touch you.

Proverbs 4:20-23

20 My son, attend to my words; incline thine ear unto my sayings. 21 Let them not depart from thine eyes; keep them in the midst of thine heart. 22 For they are life unto those that find them, and health to all their flesh. 23 Keep thy heart with all diligence; for out of it are the issues of life.

Note

Here it is as plain as it can be: the taking of God's Word is life and medicine to your flesh. So just don't take your prescribed medicine alone, take the Word of God along with it. Prescribed medicine can heal and help some things, but God's medicine can heal all.

Proverbs 16:24

Pleasant words are as an honeycomb, sweet to the soul, and health to the bones.

Note

Pleasant words, not negative words or false confessions or bad reports uttered by your mouth are sweet to your soul and bring healing. Gods word is sweet to your Spirit, Soul and Body, agree with it, confess it, talk about it even if the situation is not sweet, keep saying it and that will bring health to your bones. Imagine bones responding to spoken words, that's how powerful your own mouth is, when you agree with Gods word.

Proverbs 17:22

A merry heart doeth good like a medicine: but a broken spirit drieth the bones.

Confession: Ha, ha, ha! I have a merry heart. Sickness can't dominate me. What do you think you're trying to do, devil? You can't put sickness on me. I have a merry heart and I'm full of joy! Ha, ha, ha, ha!

Further Reading

Nehemiah 8:10

...For the joy of the LORD is your strength...

Isaiah 33:24

And the inhabitant shall not say, I am sick: the people that dwell therein shall be forgiven their iniquity.

Notice

You are an inhabitant of a country called Zion, you are not of this world, you are from above, you are the head and not from beneath. In Zion, a place of innumerable angels there is a different language from what is spoken here. They do not say 'I am sick', they hold fast to this promise and the body will fall in line with what the spirit has agreed to. Refuse sickness, walk in Divine health, it starts with a confession.

Isaiah 40:29

He giveth power to the faint; and to them that have no might he increaseth strength.

Prophetic Declaration

Today I receive Power from on high, my strength is increased by the authority of the Holy Ghost, I have the energy of God inside me, I have Gods Dunamis inside me. I refuse to be faint, weak, slow and to be in pain. My faith is increasing, my strength is increasing, I am healed in the name of Jesus Christ.

Isaiah 40:31

But they that wait upon the LORD shall renew their strength; they shall mount up

with wings as eagles; they shall run, and not be weary; and they shall walk, and not faint.

Note

The word "wait" in this verse implies a positive action of hope, based on knowing that the Word of God is a true fact and that it will soon come to pass - waiting with earnest expectation!

Isaiah 41:10

Fear thou not; for I am with thee: be not dismayed; for I am thy God: I will strengthen thee; yea, I will help thee; yea, I will uphold thee with the right hand of my righteousness.

Confession

Today I refuse to fear death, for God is with me, he is beside me and he has made me a tabernacle of his Spirit. I receive Divine Help in my time of need, I am upheld in Righteousness, I am upheld in my health, I am upheld in my strength, in the name of Jesus Christ.

Isaiah 43:25-26

25 I, even I, am he that blotteth out thy transgressions for mine own sake, and will not remember thy sins. 26 Put me in remembrance: let us plead together: declare thou, that thou mayest be justified.

Note

Your case was settled when Jesus went to the cross in your behalf! If you have accepted Jesus Christ as LORD then "It is finished!!!" Your words are important!

Isaiah 53:4-5

Surely he hath borne our griefs, and carried our sorrows: yet we did esteem him stricken, smitten of God, and afflicted. But he was wounded for our transgressions, he was bruised for our iniquities: the chastisement of our peace was upon him; and with his stripes we are healed.

Confession

Surely Jesus hath borne my sicknesses and diseases and carried my pains. He bore them and carried them away to a distance. I don't have to bear what He bore for me. I refuse to bear what He bore for me. Satan cannot put on me what Jesus bore for me. By His stripes I am healed and made whole.

Isaiah 54:17

No weapon that is formed against thee shall prosper; and every tongue that shall rise against thee in judgment thou shalt condemn. This is the heritage of the servants of the LORD, and their righteousness is of me, saith the LORD.

Note

Sickness is judging you falsely, but *it is your birthright to live in health*. You condemn it, with the Word of God, and command it to leave your body. You are an overcomer through Jesus Christ!

Isaiah 55:11

So shall my word be that goeth forth out of my mouth: it shall not return unto me void, but it shall accomplish that which I please, and it shall prosper in the thing whereto I sent it.

Note

God's Word on healing will accomplish healing in you. It will not go back void, it will accomplish your healing. Don't allow it to go back to him void, seize it as if by military force, healing is yours, prosperity is yours in your health.

Isaiah 57:19

I create the fruit of the lips; Peace, peace to him that is far off, and to him that is near, saith the LORD; and I will heal him.

Note

The word "fruit" here means produce. God creates what you produce from your mouth when we believe and speak the Word of God. Therefore agree with God and say the same that he talks about you. When you agree with him, you are taking his prescription and he will heal you.

Isaiah 58:8

Then shall thy light break forth as the morning, and thine health shall spring forth speedily: and thy righteousness shall go before thee; the glory of the LORD shall be thy rereward [protection].

Prophetic Declaration

No matter what the symptoms say, no matter what the Doctors report says, no matter what the pain is telling you, your healing, your restoration is springing forth very quickly. Supernatural Acceleration in my healing is my portion in the name of Jesus Christ.

Jeremiah 1:12

Then said the LORD unto me, Thou hast well seen: for I will hasten my word to perform it.

Note

God is looking, searching eagerly for someone to take Him at His Word so that He can perform it on their behalf. Now that you have taken your prescription, healing is yours for he is more than eager to perform it.

Jeremiah 17:14

Heal me, O LORD, and I shall be healed; save me, and I shall be saved: for thou art my praise.

Note

Once a person finally sees that healing is a finished work along with salvation, paid for at the same time with the same healing Blood, then you can get excited about this verse saying, "You did it LORD for me, then according to this verse I will agree and say I will have healing just as I have salvation, it's mine NOW!"

Jeremiah 30:17

For I will restore health unto thee, and I will heal thee of thy wounds, saith the LORD; because they called thee an Outcast, saying, This is Zion, whom no man seeketh after.

Confession

Though they have called you names, Terminally ILL, Intensive Care Patient, they may have quarantined you as an outcast, but because you are an inhabitant of Zion, healing is yours today. Your wounds are being restored, pain is going away because the Lord has said it and that settles it.

Jeremiah 33:6

Behold, I will bring it health and cure, and I will cure them, and will reveal unto them the abundance of peace and truth.

Notice the Revelation

Healing is a past tense reality, because your healing was brought at Calvary, 'by his stripes ye were healed'. It does not say, you may get healed, nor does it say you are going to be healed – NO. It says 'ye were healed', that's past tense, this is your revelation today, begin to claim this revelation, personalize it for you healing and medicine has already been brought to you over 2000 years ago

Hosea 6:1

Come, and let us return unto the LORD: for he hath torn, and he will heal us; he hath smitten, and he will bind us up.

Notice

The word return, means to come back, to reverse and revoke your old ways. Maybe your trust was on other things for your healing and nothing has happened, but if you return to the Lord by repentance and confession, he is more than willing to forgive you and give you unconditional love. He will forgive you and heal you.

Further Reading

Parable of The Prodigal Son. Luke 15: 11-32

Hosea 13:14

I will ransom them from the power of the grave; I will redeem them from death: O death, I will be thy plagues; O grave, I will be thy destruction: repentance shall be hid from mine eyes.

Prophetic Declaration: Oh Death, where is thy sting? Oh grave, where is thy victory. Death is swallowed by life, sickness is swallowed by health, I am redeemed from the power of the grave, I have been redeemed from death. I will live to testify the goodness of the Lord, in the land of the living, in the name of Jesus Christ.

Joel 3:10

Beat your plowshares into swords, and your pruning hooks into spears: let the weak say, I am strong.

Notice

Homologia, means agreeing with God, by saying the same thing that he has said, even if it contradicts your current situation. The scripture says 'let the weak', so when you are faint, weak and sick, it is not the time to say 'My Blood Pressure is high, or My cancer is growing at a faster rate' NO NO NO, it is time for you to agree, to say the same thing with God and boldly declare 'I AM STRONG'.

Malachi 4:2-3

2 But unto you that fear my name shall the Sun of righteousness arise with healing in his wings; and ye shall go forth, and grow up as calves of the stall. 3 And ye shall tread down the wicked; for they shall be ashes under the soles of your feet in the day that I shall do this, saith the LORD of hosts.

Note

I love this verse! This verse is a great promise and even tells us when it became a reality for us. "On the day that I do this" was at Calvary. Now the enemy is "ashes" under our feet and healing and protection belong to us. See Luke 10:19 also.

Do you see how loaded, Gods cabinet is, all these scripture are there for you to take in as prescription. Meditate upon them, ponder and mutter them, irrespective of the situation and if situation worsens, double the dosage.

The Key Principle

Now that you have gone through the confessions, let's look at the key principle, which makes you a partaker of God's promises concerning your healing. This is the ingredient which will make you posses the promise. Your confession must translate into possession of the promise.

You now need to act upon your healing, for you to be discharged.

FOUR

DISCHARGED: ACT UPON YOUR HEALING

Once a patient has been taking medication as prescribed, eventually the patient should be discharged. The patient should act upon the prescription, if it's to be taken after meals, you can't take the medicine before meals. You have to act upon and follow the prescription.

At times prescription goes beyond taking medicine, it may be accompanied by a change of diet or even include taking walks or exercises. Sometimes if you have been bed ridden for ages you have to go for physiotherapy, to sweat out and stretch out those muscles as you gain strength. The doctor monitors your progress up until you are discharged, thereafter your healing simply needs to be preserved and maintained.

You see confessions without possessions is faith at a junior level, your confessions is akin to taking the medicine but you then have to act upon what you believe.

Hope is a goal setter but faith is a goal getter, setting goals will not get you your healing but you have to get up and get them. Faith is acting upon what you believe. The woman with the issue of blood simply did not hold fast her confession, but she acted upon it.

The woman followed the four steps of putting your faith to work and you should too.

1. Say It.

2. Do It.

3. Receive It.

4. Tell It.

Say It

My Bible puts it this way,

> **Romans 4:17**
>
> **(As it is written, I have made thee a father of many nations,) before him whom he believed, even God, who quickeneth the dead, and calleth those things which be not as though they were.**

The scripture refers to the story of Abraham, who became fully persuaded that God would do what He had promised. He was convinced to the extent that he called those things which had not manifested in the physical as if they were. You see Abraham was called father of nations when he was still known as Abram, he was old and had no child, yet God called him a father of many nations. That was God's promise for him, that was his word and his medicine for Abram.

Abram had to agree with that word, he had to **'homologia'**, concur and say the same as God said and God taught him how to.

At first he changed his name from Abram to Abraham, which means 'father of nations', you see that, by changing his name he had to confess it, you can imagine how monotonous it was for such an Old man, when folks will call him,

'Hey, good morning Papa Abram',

and he would clear his throat, then say with an old husky voice,

'...my name is no longer Abram, it's now Abraham'.

I can imagine folks laughing and mocking him, maybe not in front him but the bold would then ask,

'why change your name now, Sir, it's been over seventy years now and you are barren'

'because, I AM Father of many nations', I imagine him answering back.

You can imagine what Abraham went through, being at pains in trying to explain his promise, from God who was not known that much then, for not much had been written about him, since Moses wrote these things in hindsight.

Abraham, stuck to his story and changed not only his name but even the name of his wife, whose womb was now medically dead for she was way past child bearing age. Each time they told people their new names, they were calling things that were not into being.

This was God's method for him to take in his medicine.

Each time they would mention his name ABRAHAM he was swallowing his pills, he was taking in God's medicine and held onto the prescription. By saying it and refusing to be called ABRAM he was calling those things that be not as if they were.

Keep telling yourself now that you are healed and continue taking the medicine as you have been doing. At the same time create faith boosters for yourself just like God created for Abraham.

God told Abraham:

"Your children shall be as the sand of the sea and as the stars of the sky..."

You see that was a faith booster to Abraham. Everytime he would go to the river or to the sea or see sand anywhere he would remember the promise. Every night when the sky is clear, he would see the stars and remember that he is healed of barrenes and would soon hold a child. It all came to pass because he had faith boosters.

I don't care what your faith booster will be but there is need for something that reminds you of God's promises.

Praying For A Man With Cancer

I remember praying for a great man of God in South Africa who had been riddled by cancer. He had helped many people receive their healing but now the devil was trying his best to kill him and render his legacy null and void. THE DEVIL WAS TRYING TO FRUSTRATE THE GRACE OF God over the man. Being a great Man of god, the devil was already celebrating because the Man Of God was now in a Wheel Chair and was preaching from one.

As I entered the house God told me to pray for thirty minutes and as I am used in the prophetic, he told me places and time when some things had happened to him. It was so detailed that it included names of people he was with and the names of countries and the locations that they were in. The man being a prophet himself knew I was hearing from God and in a way I became another **faith booster** for him.

After the thirty minutes prayer, the Lord then told me that the disease had been burnt. The cancer had left but instructed me to come back after a few weeks and I did and when I entered the house, God said "look at his walls and get into his bedroom and look at his walls and bedside."

The Man Of God being a man of the word had scripture upon scripture pinned on the walls. The house was a walking bible and he would **'homologia'** it to himself. It was encouraging. This is what the Lord had taught me and here was a man who knew it too and within four weeks the cancer that was in his blood just packed and left him. Boy I love Jesus!

The Issue of Blood

The woman with the issue of blood kept saying to herself, **'if I may touch his garment'**, this was her prescription, she kept taking her medicine. The bible puts it this way:

> **Matthew 9:21**
>
> **For she said within herself, If I may but touch his garment, I shall be whole.**

The prescription she was taking was right in the word. It means she should have read it or heard it that when the messiah comes, he will have healing in his wings, as prophesied by Malachi.

> **Malachi 4:2**
>
> **...But unto you that fear my name shall the Sun of righteousness arise with healing in his wings...**

You see, faith cometh by hearing, and hearing by the word of God. She read or heard it from the scrolls of Malachi and she received her faith. By saying it she was now calling the things which be not as if they were. For she said 'I shall be whole', she was calling forth her healing. She could picture it and imagine it, she could have made a negative confession because the Bible says:

Mark 5:26

And had suffered many things of many physicians, and had spent all that she had, and was nothing bettered, but rather grew worse,

You can imagine her frustrations, Doctors couldn't help her, her cash had run out, her situation was getting worse. Remember our prescription, when the situation gets worse, double the dosage. She could have said, 'there is no use for me to go, I have suffered for twelve whole years, the doctors have given up on me, I have spent all in consultations, seeing general practitioners and even specialists, now I don't even have anything for medical Aid. I am getting worse, I might as well just die.

You see, you reap what you sow, 'seed time and harvest, shall not cease, as long as the earth remains'. Words are seeds and you reap what you sow. Instead she took her medicine, she maintained a positive confession, for she said '*If I may but touch his garment, I shall be whole*'. She held fast onto her prescription. You have to SAY IT.

Do It

There are two parts to everything you receive from God: The part God plays and the part you play. God is not going to fail in doing his part. If you do your part, you can be sure of an answer and victory.

God has sent his word, His medicine which is your prescription, that way He has done his part. Your part is to take the medicine as per prescription and act upon it. The woman with the issue of blood just did not confess the word, for confession without possession is faith at a junior level, she had to act upon it. Remember as alluded to earlier, she had many obstacles against her. There was a multitude which thronged Jesus and the Law of Moses was clear about women with issue of blood, but this was not sufficient to deter her, she was not a hearer but a doer of the word.

Crowd or no crowd, Mosaic Law or no Law, in her weakened state and broke state she set out to do what she confessed. She acted upon what she believed, she put action into her words and she did the extraordinary.

Luke 8:44

...Came behind him, and touched the border of his garment...

She did not follow diplomacy or protocol; she did not have a front door policy. She sneaked from behind and touched the garment with her medicine. Her faith did not end with confessions, it did not end with meditation of the word. SHE ACTED UPON IT.

Say it. Do it, and now.

Receive It

The Bible says, when she touched the garment, something happened, she received something:

Luke 8:44

...And IMMEDIATELY her issue of blood stanched...

Mark narrates it this way:

Mark 5:29

And STRAIGHTAWAY the fountain of her blood was dried up; and she felt in her body that she was healed of that plague.

The word of God will never return to him void, what Malachi had prophesied 400 years earlier came alive. This was because she decided to act upon her healing. She took her prescription and put it to use. You can be given capsules from the pharmacy and choose not to swallow them, she grabbed her medicine from the garment and received her healing. She did something for her to receive her healing, she acted upon it, and by touching the garment she was able to draw out her miracle. The point of contact became a conductor to draw out her healing. Now remember there was a crowd which thronged Jesus. Watch this:

Luke 8:45-46

And Jesus said, Who touched me? When all denied, Peter and they that were with him said, Master, the multitude throng thee and press thee, and sayest thou, Who touched me? And Jesus said, Somebody hath touched me: for I perceive that virtue is gone out of me.

I want you to notice something. The Bible in Mark 5:29 says:

"she felt within herself that she was healed..."

This denotes that she believed that she was healed even before she checked the results. Remember the woman had suffered for 12 years so it is reasonable to assume that she was not bleeding consistently otherwise she would have died of loss of blood. She also could not check herself because she would have had to remove her clothes to check so:

"she felt within herself..."

Agree that you are healed. **Here I am not saying don't take your medicine from your doctor. Take it hand in hand. Remember its not God who said you were sick**. It is the doctor who said it and gave you medicine so he is the one to go back to for further check up. Let him be the one to check you. You simply have to believe you are healed because you will be. God's medicine works.

The woman received something and Jesus felt something, Peter interjected amongst denials and said what he found to be reasonable. A lot of people were in contact with Jesus, because they 'thronged and pressed' yet none of them received anything except for the woman with the issue of blood. You see you can come to the Doctors medical chamber, have a consultation with him, sitting face to face with him and yet not receive anything from him. You can even go out thinking, he is a bad doctor yet the next patient after you receives her healing. Many were in touch with Jesus, perhaps others even touched the hem of his garment yet did not receive anything.

The anointing is a heavenly materiality, which is transferable, but for you to receive you have to plug in and switch on. By the same token, electricity is an earthly materiality, for you to receive you have to plug in and it becomes transferable if there is a conductor. The conductor for supernatural power is faith. Jesus felt power coming out, yet when others touched him he didn't feel anything coming out. Watch this:

Matthew 9:22

...But Jesus turned him about, and when he saw her, he said, Daughter, be of good comfort; thy faith hath made thee whole...

Now some folks say, why isn't everyone healed, there you have it, Jesus said **'thy faith hath made thee whole'**, he didn't say **'the virtue that I felt out',** he said **'thy faith'** referring to the woman's faith, not the faith of Jesus. Virtue, dunamis, dynamic and inherent healing power is what Jesus carried, but it takes faith to conduct it and draw it out for you to receive your healing. Many people touched Jesus, but only one had the faith to draw out the medicine from the cabinet. Healing power will flow towards where there is faith.

Faith is the conductor which draws it out, you see God has already done everything he can do for you, he has sent his word, his medicine and his medicine will not return void. He has already done something about it, it's now up to you to receive it. You have to get into the cabinet, take the medicine and swallow it, it needs your action which is your faith. Now that you have acted upon it and have received it, there is one more step to do.

Tell It

Can I testify?

Testify!

The Bible puts it this way:

> **Revelation 12:9-11**
>
> **And the great dragon was cast out, that old serpent, called the Devil, and Satan, which deceiveth the whole world: he was cast out into the earth, and his angels were cast out with him. And I heard a loud voice saying in heaven, Now is come salvation, and strength, and the kingdom of our God, and the power of his Christ: for the accuser of our brethren is cast down, which accused them before our God day and night. And they overcame him by the blood of the Lamb, and by THE WORD OF THEIR TESTIMONY and they loved not their lives unto the death.**

The devil, Satan, came to steal, kill and destroy. Salvation came with power by the blood of the lamb, Jesus Christ.

Salvation includes your healing, for the Bible says 'by his stripes, ye were healed', the blood of the lamb was shed for you to be delivered from the Kingdom of the devil to the Kingdom of Light, which is the Kingdom of God. God has done his part by overcoming the ACCUSER by the blood of the lamb but you now have to do your part which is 'Telling it', testifying your healing miracle. Notice, the devil was described as 'that serpent of old', if you don't tell it, if you don't testify the serpent will grow into a dragon.

Remember the story of the 10 lepers who got cleansed of leprosy as they went to the priest, yet only one came back and Jesus said:

Luke 17:15-19

And one of them, when he saw that he was healed, turned back, and with a loud voice glorified God, And fell down on his face at his feet, giving him thanks: and he was a Samaritan. And Jesus answering said, Were there not ten cleansed? but where are the nine? There are not found that returned to give glory to God, save this stranger. And he said unto him, Arise, go thy way: thy faith hath made thee whole.

Only one, came back to 'Tell it' glorified God, yet ten lepers were cleansed. With a loud voice he told his testimony, he gave Jesus thanks. When we glorify God we render him glorious, we magnify and honour him. It's to give him praise and thanks with excitement so as to make it known to the world that if it wasn't for God, it wasn't going to be possible that my healing has come.

Notice ten lepers were cleansed but only one was made whole, being cleansed means the disease was removed but after one testified, he was made whole. Being made whole means to be made sound and kept safe. That is how you maintain your healing, you keep testifying your miracle, keep telling it, keep glorifying God and no matter how much the devil tries to fight your testimony, keep testifying, keep telling it.

Do you know that doctors are guided by strong ethics; they are not allowed to openly market their work. They rely on one thing and one thing alone. They rely on referrals, when a patient has been given a good service they refer others to their doctor. The great physician also wants your testimony to be told so that all glory due unto him accrues to him, also your testimony will raise someone's faith to receive their own healing and a lot of souls have been won to Christ because of testimonies of the saints.

The woman with the issue of blood, did not steal God's glory, she came back to **'Tell It'**.

My Bible puts it this way:

Mark 5:32-33

And he looked round about to see her that had done this thing. But the woman fearing and trembling, knowing what was done in her, came and fell down before him, and told him all the truth.

There was a multitude, so the disciples couldn't see who had drawn out virtue out of Jesus. Jesus felt something and looked around. She could have sneaked away because in the first place she was not supposed to be there because of cultural reasons. She did come back to 'Tell it' and the whole crowd heard it. She told him all the truth, testimony is when you tell what happened, which is different from the first step, where you are saying what you believe by confessing.

These four steps are applicable as a prescription not only for healing but even for deliverance, victory over sin, victory over the devil and even over finances. **Say it, Do it, Receive it and Tell it.**

Healing is yours today, God has sent his word, he has sent his medicine, he has shown you his medicine cabinet, it's up to you to take the particular medicine which pertains to your situation. Take the medicine and swallow it, meditate upon his word day and night. Visualize your healing, say it, call for it, call things that be not as if they were.

Exercise your faith, put it to work, grow your faith, move it from small faith to great faith. Faith is a seed, though being small it can move mountains, no sickness can stand in your way, no disease can't be healed, your faith is a conductor to draw out your healing which was delivered to you at Calvary. Receive your healing now and testify the goodness of the Lord.

The Word of God, is your Medicine, if conceived in the human spirit by meditation and formed by the tongue and spoken out it becomes the present reality of your healing today.

Repeat the dosage daily and you will see the results!

If extreme pain persists rush to the ER which will deal with your emergency symptoms in Chapter FIVE. RUSH THERE NOW!

FIVE
EMERGENCY ROOMS

Emergency Rooms are hospital room or area equipped and staffed by professionals for the reception and treatment of persons requiring immediate medical care.

God has his own Emergency Rooms for immediate care for his loved ones. It is well prepared with the right equipment and professional staff.

Emergency Rooms – Equipment – Praying in Tongues

Typically emergency rooms have resuscitators so as to revive and revitalize ER cases. God's ER has a good resuscitator – it's called speaking in tongues. Apostle Paul gives us an expose!

1 Corinthians 14:18

I thank my God, I speak with tongues more than ye all:

You may be forgiven for thinking that Apostle Paul was boasting right there, but Apostle Paul had discovered a secret about praying in tongues. There just has to be something about tongues for him to go to the extent of saying I thank God 'I speak in tongues more than you all'. You see prayer can be done with understanding or in the spirit, where the spirit lead you to break into unknown tongues punctuated with groaning's which cannot be uttered. You should do more of praying in tongues than praying with understanding, for praying in tongues is Spirit led. Watch this:

1 Corinthians 14:15

What is it then? I will pray with the spirit, and I will pray with the understanding ALSO: I will sing with the spirit, and I will sing with the understanding also.

Do you notice his secret right there. The key word is 'also', he gives priority to praying in the spirit, then he says 'and I will pray with understanding also'. This means there is something about praying in tongues, which is to your advantage. Notice:

1 Corinthians 14:4

He that speaketh in an unknown tongue edifieth himself; but he that prophesieth edifieth the church.

Do you see the advantage of speaking in unknown tongues, the God's word, his medicine says if you do so you 'edify yourself'. Now the word edify is the word **'oikodomeo'.** In the Greek rendering, The word means, you have become a builder, who is restoring, rebuilding and renovating a building. Now your body is the temple of the Lord. You also stay in your body as the spirit, inner man. When your body has been destroyed by sickness, disease and infirmity don't cry brother, don't cry sister you have your own supernatural Cardiopulmonary Resuscitation (CPR – emergency rooms jump starters) in built in your spirit, you have to take it out by praying in tongues. Praying in tongues repairs your temple, your body, when you speak in tongues disease begins to check out and if done consistently not only will you maintain your healing but you will prevent any other diseases from even stepping into your temple.

Make it a point to pray in the spirit every day and pray with understanding also. It secures your health and attunes your spirit to the ordering of your steps by the Lord.

In the Emergency Rooms there are also professional staff who attend to emergency cases. You see a hospital has general practitioners and specialists who operate in special areas like Emergency Rooms.

Emergency Rooms – Professional Staff – Gifts of Healings

God has made the Holy Spirit available to every believer and there are promises which come with it. Notice, there is the commission and special offices. The commission is akin to general practitioners but there are offices where there are specialists. Take a close look at this:

Mark 16:17-18

And these signs shall follow them that believe; In my name shall they cast out devils; they shall speak with new tongues; They shall take up serpents; and if they drink any deadly thing, it shall not hurt them; they shall lay hands on the sick, and they shall recover.

Notice that is available to every believer, in the name of Jesus you can lay hands on the sick and they will recover. That's part of the commission, available to every believer, akin to general practitioners but there are also specialists in this big Hospital of God. Watch this:

1 Corinthians 12:27-30

Now ye are the body of Christ, and members in particular. And God hath set some in the church, first apostles, secondarily prophets, thirdly teachers, after that miracles, then gifts of healings, helps, governments, diversities of tongues. Are all apostles? are all prophets? are all teachers? are all workers of miracles? Have all the gifts of healing? do all speak with tongues? do all interpret?

Now watch this, over and above what is available to every believer, there is something which God, by election of grace has given to some, not all. It says 'God has set some', how he set them it's by grace, you do not choose to become a Prophet, its God who sets an office and anoint a person as a vessel for that particular office. Notice it says 'gifts of healings', it says it in the plural not in a singular which means in the Office of healing there are particular specialists for specific ailments in as much as you have general practitioners and specialists in a hospital. He then asks a rhetoric question, 'are all apostles? Are all prophets? Are all teachers? Have all gifts of healings? The answer is an eloquent NO.

There are people who have been called by God by election by grace, unmerited favour who have been given particular offices to edify the body of Christ. Gifts of healings come with it.

By his grace my wife and I, have been given grace in the office of the prophetic and gifts of healings as well inter alia. You see the prophetic office enables us to scan a pregnancy, determine age and sex, just by looking at someone we can tell the ailment which is affecting someone and even to the extent of seeing death whilst someone is still walking. We give God glory for such grace, and my God reveals in order to redeem. When he reveals it means he is more than willing to solve the problems. We have had many healing testimonies, including resurrections from death by the authority of the Holy Ghost and in the name of Jesus Christ BUT ALL OF THEM CAME BECAUSE OF UNDERSTANDING GOD'S MEDICINE and not just because of the PROPHETIC in our lives.

We give God glory that he has a healing agent for you.

For healing to be quick connect with other people that believe in healing. Be part of a church that believes in DOCTOR JESUS. Connect with Man Of God who can encourage you and feed you extra dose.

Such professionals, who have been anointed for such specific work by the Lord have been made available for you, go and connect with such anointing, go in faith and receive your miracle and more importantly maintain that healing and keep it. Remember what the Bible says:

Matthew 12:43-45

When the unclean spirit is gone out of a man, he walketh through dry places, seeking rest, and findeth none.

Then he saith, I will return into my house from whence I came out; and when he is come, he findeth it empty, swept and garnished.

Then goeth he, and taketh with himself, seven other spirits more wicked than himself, and they enter in and dwell there: and the last state of that man is worse than the first.

So you see that it is possible to lose your healing after getting it, yet God's plan for you is that you keep your healing and that you don't get sick. He wants you to enjoy divine healing and divine health. Partake from his medicine cabinet, meditate upon his word – swallow his medicine, act upon what you believe and connect with his anointed servants.

Jesus is the Healer, Jesus is the word – He is your DOCTOR and His word is your medicine.

Jesus wants to heal you today. Receive your healing in the name of Jesus!

ABOUT THE AUTHOR

Widely known around the world as the Godfather of the modern-day Prophetic movement, Uebert Angel presides over an ever-widening number of The GoodNews Church (Spirit Embassy) branches worldwide. Uebert Angel has touched the lives of millions through his satellite-broadcasting channels, Miracle TV, GoodNews TV and Wow TV, which broadcast his remarkable Healing, Prophetic and Revelatory Teaching ministry 24 hours-7 days a week around the globe, books, magazines, charity programmes, conferences and crusades.

He is also the author of many bestsellers, including *How to Hear The Voice of God, Defeating The Demon of Poverty*, and the daily devotional *The GoodNews Daily*, which he co-authors with his wife, BeBe Angel. Through an anointed ministry now synonymous with miracles, signs, wonders and accurate prophecies, Uebert Angel has helped many receive healings and miracles.

He is also a Forbes featured businessman and Zimbabwe's first Presidential Envoy and Ambassador-At-Large, responsible for over 85 countries. As a British National, he is educated in Great Britain with a Master's Degree in Entrepreneurship from Edinburgh University (Napier), a degree in Business and Finance from Salford University, and a Post-Graduate Degree in Education from University of Bolton.

Connect with His Excellency Ambassador Uebert Angel at
uebertangel.org

ALSO BY UEBERT ANGEL

How to Hear the Voice of God

Defeating the Demon of Poverty

Becoming A Millionaire in Real Estate

Provoking the Angels of Money

God's Get Rich Quick Scheme

The Greatest Secret God Told Me About Money

Genetics of Words

Prayer Banks

The Prayer that God Cannot Ignore

Hello Holy Spirit

Spiritual Warfare

I Went to Hell

The Money Is Coming

Available at:

uebertangel.org

Amazon.com

Wherever Books Are Sold

Lightning Source UK Ltd.
Milton Keynes UK
UKHW020250011022
409720UK00011B/670